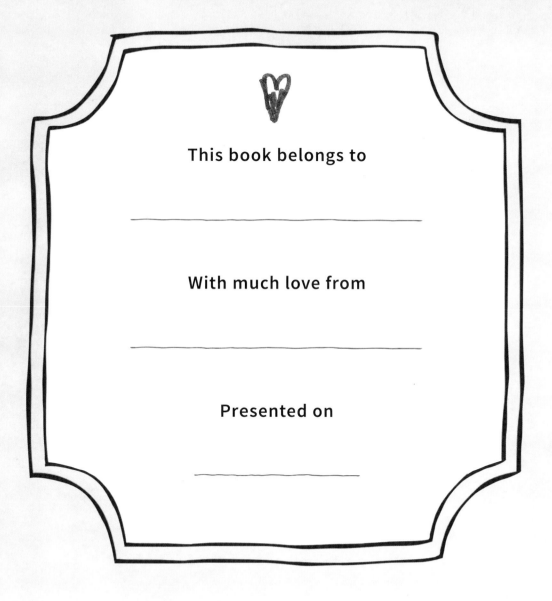

This book belongs to

_____

With much love from

_____

Presented on

_____

Dear Pope Francis

By Pope Francis and the Children of the World

In conversation with Antonio Spadaro, S.J.

Project Managing Editor, Tom McGrath

LOYOLAPRESS.
A JESUIT MINISTRY

Chicago

LOYOLA PRESS.
A JESUIT MINISTRY

3441 N. Ashland Avenue
Chicago, Illinois 60657
(800) 621-1008
www.loyolapress.com

© 2016 Libreria Editrice Vaticana
00120 Città del Vaticano
www.libreriaeditricevaticana.com

Author: Pope Francis

Edited by: Antonio Spadaro, S.J., *La Civiltà Cattolica*

Project Managing Editor: Tom McGrath, Loyola Press

Cover design: Jill Arena, Loyola Press

Production artist: Becca Gay, Loyola Press

Illustrations: Children of the world

Front cover illustration: Judith from Belgium, age 9

Back cover illustration: Janice from China, age 7

Image credits: L'Osservatore Romano (p 69); iStock.com/donatas1205 (endsheet); iStock.com/iconeer (pp 70–71)

ISBN-13: 978-0-8294-4433-9
ISBN-10: 0-8294-4433-5

Library of Congress Control Number: 2015956752

Printed in the United States of America

15 16 17 18 19 20 21 22 Bang 10 9 8 7 6 5 4 3 2 1

of the world

Thank you for sending me your letters.

It brings me joy to read them all.

Franciscus

Dear Pope Francis,

When I saw you at St. Peter's Square, I felt great joy when you looked at me. What do you feel when you look at the children around you? Thank you for your attention.

A hug from João

Age 10, Portugal

Querido Papa Francisco,

Quando o vi na Praça de São Pedro senti uma grande alegria porque olhou para mim. O que sente quando olha para as crianças à sua volta?

Obrigado pela sua atenção.

Um abraço do João.

Dear João,

You asked me what I feel when I look at children. I do see many children! I smile at them and hug them and throw kisses from the car, because my hands are free—even though you drew me with my hands on the wheel!

I'm happy when I see children. I always feel great tenderness and affection for them. But it's more than that. Actually, when I look at a child like you, I feel great hope rising in my heart. Because, for me, seeing a child is seeing the future. Yes, I feel great hope because every child is our hope for the future of humanity.

Franciscus

Dear Pope Francis,

I would like to know more about Jesus Christ. How did he walk on water?

Love,
Natasha

Age 8, Kenya

Dear Pope Francis,
I would like to know more about Jesus Christ. How did he walk on water?

Love ❤
Natasha.

Dear Natasha,

You have to imagine Jesus walking naturally, normally. He did not fly over the water or turn somersaults while swimming. He walked as you walk! He walked, one foot after the other, as if the water were land. He walked on the water's surface as he saw the fish under his feet frolicking or racing around.

Jesus is God, and so he can do anything! He can walk safely on water. God cannot sink, you know!

Franciscus

Dear Pope Francis,

Our deceased relatives, can they see us from heaven?

Emil

*Age 9,
Dominican Republic*

Querido Papa Francisco:

Nuestros familiares fallecidos, ¿Pueden vernos desde el cielo?

Emil

Dear Emil,

Yes, you can be sure of this. I imagine that you're thinking about your relatives who are in heaven. You don't see them, but—if and when God allows it—they can see you, at least in certain moments of your life. They are not far from us, you know? They pray for us, and they lovingly take care of us. This is the important thing.

You can imagine your deceased relatives this way: they are smiling down on you from heaven. The way you have drawn them, they are flying around me. But they are "flying" next to you. They are accompanying you with their love.

Franciscus

Dear Pope Francis,

It's an honour to ask you my question. My question is, what did God do before the world was made?

Sincerely,
Ryan

Age 8, Canada

Dear pope Francis

It's an honour to ask you my question. My question is what did God do before the world was made?

Sincerely,
Ryan

12

Dear Ryan,

There is beauty in creation. And there are the limitless and eternal tenderness and mercy of God. God began making something when he created the world. But if I told you that God was doing nothing before he created the world, I would be wrong. In fact, God also created time—that is, the "before" and the "after." But I don't want to confuse you with these words. Think of it this way: before creating anything, God loved. That's what God was doing: God was loving. God always loves. God *is* love. So when God began making the world, he was simply expressing his love. Before doing anything else, God was love, and God was loving.

Franciscus

Dear Pope Francis,

Where is your favourite place to pray, and why?

From Josephine

Age 8, United Kingdom

Dear Pope Francis,

Where is your favourite place to pray, and why?

From Josephine.

Dear Josephine,

You know, I like to pray everywhere. I can even pray at my desk or in my armchair in the living room. Many times in the evening I'm tired, so I don't go down to the chapel but stay in my room and pray. I love to be in church in front of the Most Blessed Sacrament. I do that often. I very much like to go there and sit in silence before God. But I can also pray while walking, or even when I go to the dentist. I find God everywhere.

Franciscus

Dear Pope Francis,

You are not very young anymore, and you have already done many things. What more do you want to do in your life to make the world more beautiful and fair?

Greetings,
Hannes and Lidewij

Age 9, twins from the Netherlands

Art translation:
Past, Present, Future

Beste Paus Franciscus,

U bent al best wel oud en u heeft al heel veel gedaan. Wat wilt u nog doen in uw leven om de wereld mooier en eerlijker te maken?

Groeten,

Hannes en Lidewij

verleden   Heden   Toekomst

Dear Hannes and Lidewij,

There are so many things I would like to do. I would like to smile always—smile at God first of all to thank him for all the good he does for people. I would like to thank God for his patience. Have you ever thought about how much patience God has? God is very patient. God waits and waits for us.

I want to help the people who suffer. I would like to make sure that there are no more injustices or at least that there are not so many of them. I want to help children get to know Jesus. I wish there were no longer any slaves in this world. There are still many slaves in this world—so many. I desire to do all this, but I am old and I have very little thread left in the spool so...God will tell...

Franciscus

Your Holiness,

Will my grandpa, a non-Catholic who is not a person willing to do something evil, go to heaven when he dies? In other words, if someone never makes any penances, how big a sin must he commit for him to go down to Hell?

God bless you,
Ivan

Age 13, China

我的爷爷不信天主，但他也不会做什么坏事，他是会上天堂吗？亦或是一个人在没有忏悔的情况下，犯了多大的错，才会下地狱呢？

天主保佑！✝

— 梵 Ivan

Dear Ivan,

Jesus loves us so very much, and he wants all of us to go to heaven. God's will is that everybody would be saved. Jesus walks with us until the very last moment of our lives, so that we can be with him always. Now appearances can certainly deceive us. For example, some people think that because you don't follow every Church rule to the letter, you will automatically go to hell. But in fact, Jesus is beside us throughout our lives—to the very last moment!—to save us.

Once, a woman went to a holy priest whose name was John Maria Vianney. He was the pastor of the parish in Ars, in France. The woman began to cry, because her husband had committed suicide by jumping off a bridge. She was desperate because she thought that her husband had certainly ended up in hell. But Father John Maria, who was a saint, said to her, "Look, between the bridge and the river, there is the mercy of God."

Franciscus

Dear Pope Francis,

When you were a child, did you like dancing?

Prajla

Age 6, Albania

PRAJLA

Kur ishe ſëmijë të pëlgente të Kërceje?

Very much, dear Prajla!

Really a lot! I enjoyed being with other children, playing Ring around the Rosie, but also dancing our traditional dances from Argentina. I really had so much fun! Then, as a young man, I liked to dance the tango. I really like the tango. You know, dancing expresses joy and happiness. When you are sad, you can't dance. Usually, young people have one great resource: being happy. And for this reason, when you are young, you dance and express the joy in your heart.

Even the great King David danced. He made Jerusalem the Holy City and brought the Ark of the Covenant there in a solemn procession. And then King David began to dance in front of the Ark. He didn't worry about formality. He forgot to behave as a king, and he began to dance like a little child! But when his wife, Michal, saw him jumping and dancing, she criticized David and scorned him in her heart. She was sick with too much seriousness, what I call the "Michal Syndrome." People who can't express joy are always serious. Dance now, children, so you won't be too serious when you grow up!

Franciscus

21

Dear Pope Francis,

If God loves us so much and didn't want us to suffer, why didn't he defeat the devil?

From Alejandra

Age 9, Peru

Image of angels translation:
God, The Fans

Querido Papa Francisco

¿Si Dios nos ama tanto y no quiere que suframos, por qué no derrotó al Diablo?

De: Alejandra

Dear Alejandra,

God *has* defeated the devil, and he did it on the Cross. He defeated the devil, but in his own way. The devil is a loser and has been defeated. Do you know how dragons are? They have a very long tail, and even if they have been killed, they continue to shake that tail for a while. What happened to the devil is like what happens to big and scary dragons that are defeated and killed. Their long tail moves and can still cause damage. In a small way, you can see it with little lizards when they lose their tails. Even though the tail is detached from the body, it continues to shake. Jesus' death defeated death. The devil is a loser—don't forget it! He is like a dragon or a dangerous dinosaur that wags its tail for a while even if it's already dead.

Or, here's another image: the devil is like a dog that is tied up and barks and growls. But if you don't get close to him, he can't bite you.

Franciscus

Dear Pope Francis,

What makes you happy in your work as pope?

Judith

Age 9, Belgium

Beste Paus Franciscus,
Wat maakt u gelukkig
in uw werk als paus?
Judith

Dear Judith,

It makes me happy to be with people. That is what makes me happy. If I cannot be with people, I spend time with Jesus and talk to him about people. I can't imagine myself alone.

Judith, I like your drawing. I think of myself as you have drawn me: hand in hand with you and your friends. Being together with others brings me joy. And as the pope, I think I ought to be with people.

Franciscus

Querido Papa Francisco,

¿ Por qué Jesús eligió a esos 12 apóstoles y no a otros?

Besos, Juan Pablo

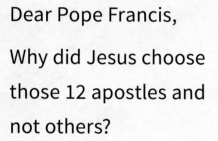

Dear Pope Francis,

Why did Jesus choose those 12 apostles and not others?

Kisses,
Juan Pablo

Age 10, Argentina, pictured with his sister, Carolina

Great question, dear Juan Pablo!

Why does Jesus choose this person or that one? Look, Jesus doesn't choose a crowd. He chooses each person, one by one. So he chose the first twelve as his apostles. But we—you and I—are also chosen, with a first name and a family name. I have been chosen as Jorge Mario and you as Juan Pablo. We have been chosen to be Jesus' friends and to do something in life.

We are all chosen by the love of Jesus. But each of us is chosen in a personal way—we are not all chosen in a single common way. Jesus' love makes us feel chosen. But if you feel shut out of this love, then you have to face up to it and ask yourself why you feel that way. Jesus never excludes anyone from his heart. The red heart you drew is beautiful!

Franciscus

Dear Pope Francis,

I hope you read my letter. I wanted to see you ever since I heard about you. Pope Francis, do you know why some parents argue with each other?

Love,
Alexandra

Age 10, Philippines

Dear Pope Francis,

I hope you read my letter. I wanted to see you eversince I heard about you. Pope Francis, do you know why some parents argue each other?

Love, Alexandra

me

pope Francis

Dear Alexandra,

We all argue. We are all human. Even I have argued. Our life together always has its problems. You shouldn't be surprised by this. It's normal. I like one thing, and you like something else. At times, we find ourselves in disagreement. Even you, I am sure, argue once in a while with your friends. But life goes on, and we move forward. We overcome difficulties together. It's normal for people to argue. And so your parents argue, too.

But there is a sort of magic formula to solve these disagreements—did you know that? Parents must try never to end the day without making peace. If you carry anger and sadness inside of you at night, you will get up in the morning with a cold heart that won't easily warm up. In your drawing, there's you and there's me. We're smiling. There's a rainbow that comes out from the clouds, and so does the sun. This is peace! If you want to help your parents, I advise you, most of all, not to talk badly about your dad to your mom, and not to talk badly about your mom to your dad. Stay close to your mom and dad and speak well of them. That will be good for everyone.

Franciscus

Dear Pope Francis,

How can God hear us?

God bless you!

Love,
Ryan

Age 7,
United States of America

Drawing of Ryan's Baptism

Do you know, Ryan, that God listens to us?

Yes, he listens to us, but not with ears. God can hear us
even if words don't come out of our mouths. God listens
to the heart. Jesus also said this: When we pray, we
don't have to say many things; we don't have to have
long discussions with God. They aren't needed. What we
need to do, however, is to really open our hearts to him.
We must open our hearts just as they are. Then God can
listen to what we have in our hearts. And Jesus, because
he is God, is near to every person and listens to everyone.
He is God, and he can do this.

Franciscus

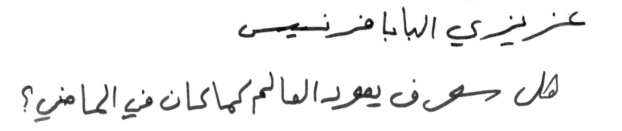

Dear Pope Francis,

Will the world be again as it was in the past?

Respectfully yours, Mohammed

Age 10, Syria

Dear Mohammed,

We believe that Jesus came to save us and that he has defeated the devil. But he also promised us that he would come back. We are waiting for him. And the Bible says that when he returns, everything will be new: a new heaven and a new earth. No, when that time comes, the world will not be as it was. It will be far better than it was in the past. In today's world there is so much suffering. And, unfortunately, you know that firsthand. There are those who manufacture weapons so that people fight each other and wage war. There are people who have hate in their hearts. There are people who are interested only in money and would sell everything for it. They would even sell other people. This is terrible. This is suffering.

But, you know, this suffering is destined to end. It is not forever. Suffering is to be lived with hope. We are not prisoners of suffering. It is just as you have expressed in your drawing: with the sun, the flowers, the trees, and your smile as you fly in the air playing ball. If we forgive one another, we will go to our future home, which will be very beautiful because it will be transfigured—completely transformed—by the presence of God.

Franciscus

Dear Pope Francis,

Do you feel like a father to everyone?

Yours considered,
Clara

Age 11, Ireland

A Phápa Proinsias, a chara,
An airíonn tú mar Phápa gur tú athair ag an domhain iomlán?
mise le Mheas
Clara

Dear Clara,

Every priest likes to feel that he is a father.
Spiritual fatherhood is truly important. I feel it
deeply: I couldn't think of myself in any other
way except as a father. And I very much like your
drawing with a big heart in which there's a dad with
two little girls. Are you the one with the teddy bear?
Yes, Clara, I like being a dad.

Franciscus

Dear Pope Francis,

I am very interested in writing to you and everything related to the Catholic world. I have always asked myself: Do bad people have a guardian angel, too?

With lots of love,
Karla Marie

Age 10, Nicaragua

Querido papa Francisco,

Estoy muy interesada en escribirte esta carta y en todo lo catolico. Siempre me he pregontado algo. ¿Quisiera saber si las personas malas tambien tienen ángel de la guardia?

Con mucho cariño,
Karla

Dear Karla,

We all have a guardian angel! One way to help people who are doing bad things is to pray to their guardian angels so their angels can help them do what is good. Another thing you can do is pray to your own guardian angel so that he becomes friends with the guardian angel of a person who is doing wrong. That person's angel can urge him to come to his senses. Children should realize that every person—bad or good—has a guardian angel to pray to so that their angels can take care of them. God gives us angels to help us improve, change, and become people who do what pleases God.

Guardian angels accompany people who do wrong. The angels try to help them realize their mistakes and where they are not on the right path. Our angels help us think good thoughts and, in general, they take care of us. Of course, some people don't always listen to their guardian angels. And some almost never listen. Still, their angel always accompanies them—*always*.

Franciscus

Dear Pope Francis,

Why do you think children have to go to Catechesis [religious education]? I liked when you appeared on the flyer for the Fraternity Campaign. Come again to Brazil. I would like to see you.

A hug and a kiss,
Ana Maria

Age 10, Brazil

Querido Papa Francisco

Porque você acha que as Crianças devem fazer Catequese?

Eu gosto quando você aparece no cartaz da Companha da fraternidade.

Venha mais uma vez ao Brasil, gostaria de te ver.

Um abraço e um beijo,
Ana

Dear Ana,

You go to catechism to get to know Jesus better! If you have a friend, you enjoy being with him and getting to know him better. You enjoy being with your friend, playing together and getting to know his family, his life, where he was born, and where he lives. This is a good thing. Religious education classes help you get to know your friend Jesus better and his great family, the Church.

There are many ways to get acquainted with Jesus. Actually, you don't so much learn about Jesus as go in search of him so you can meet him as a person. When you look for Jesus, he will come to you and help you get to know him.

I have to tell you something: You can know many things about Jesus, but that's not enough. You may also know his story, all that he has done, but you don't get to know Jesus just by studying him. You come to know Jesus by reading the Gospel, praying, seeking him in all you do, doing good to those who are in need, and helping the sick. If you do this, Jesus will surely come close so that you can meet him and know him.

Franciscus

Dear Pope Francis,

My mum is in Heaven.

Will she grow angel wings?

From LUCA

Dear Pope Francis,

My mum is in heaven. Will she grow angel wings?

From Luca

Age 7, Australia

Dear Luca,

No, no, no! Your mom is in heaven—beautiful, splendid, and full of light. She hasn't grown wings. She is still your mom, the person you know, but she is more radiant than ever. And she watches you and smiles at you as her son. Your mom is happy whenever she sees you behaving well. And if you don't behave, she still loves you and asks Jesus to help you become a better person.

Think of your mother like this: beautiful, smiling, and full of love for you.

Franciscus

Dear Pope Francis,

What was your hardest choice in your mission for faith?

From,
Tom

Age 8, United Kingdom

Dear Pope Francis,

What was your hardest choice in your misson for faith?

From,

Tom

Dear Tom,

You're asking a question that isn't easy. In your drawing, there's a question mark. There are so many difficult choices, but if I have to name the most difficult, the toughest choice, it would be this: it is when I have to let someone go. What I mean is, sometimes I have to take someone away from a certain job or responsibility. Or I have to remove them from a position of trust or from a special role that isn't right for them.

Letting people go is really very difficult for me. I love to trust people. And that's true for those I work with and anyone I'm responsible for. So I feel really bad if I have to send someone away. But at times I have to do it, you know, for the good of the person. Still, it's difficult for me to accept.

Franciscus

Dear Pope Francis,

Why do you like to play soccer?

Wishing you good health.

Wing

Age 8, China

Dear Wing,

I really like soccer. I have never played serious matches because I never learned the art of the game that well. I don't have a nimble foot. But I really do like watching the teams play on the field. Do you know why? Because I see teamwork and unity.

I get excited watching a match. If a player wants to play all by himself, he loses, and then his teammates will not like him. To play soccer well, you must play together. You must play as a team and look for the good of everyone without thinking about your personal gain or showing off. It ought to be this way in the Church too!

Franciscus

Dear Pope Francis,

Why are lots of people so poor and have no food? Can God give the poor people some food like he fed the 5000 people?

Love from Thierry

Age 7, Australia

Dear Pope Francis,

why are lots of people so poor and have No food? can God give the poor people Some food like He fed the 5000 people?

Love from Thierry

Yes, yes! He can do that, Thierry!

And he continues to do so. At that time, Jesus gave bread to the disciples to distribute to all the people. If Jesus' disciples had not passed out the food, the people would have still been hungry. See, there is bread! And there is enough for everyone! The real problem is that some of those who have plenty do not want to share it with others. The problem is not Jesus, but the mean and selfish people who want to keep their abundance all for themselves. With these people, Jesus is very stern. We have to learn to share our wealth and the food we have. That way, there will be enough for all, and everyone will be happy.

Franciscus

Dear Pope Francis,

Why do we venerate the Cross?

How are you? I am fine.

Yours,
Tadiwanashe

Age 10, Zimbabwe

Kuna Papa

Ndanyora tsamba iyi ndichida kukubvunzai mubvunzo unoti nemhaka yei tichipfugamira chipiyaniso?

Makadii henyu? Ini ndinofora

Ndini wenyu

Tadiwanashe

Dear Tadiwanashe,

We venerate, or honor, the Cross because Saint Paul says that the Cross is our glory. The Cross is the place where Jesus won and achieved his victory over evil and death. In the Olympics, winners are placed on a higher step and given a beautiful trophy. In this case, Jesus' trophy is his Cross, his triumph. With his death on the Cross, Jesus conquered death. He won! The Cross is the sign of this victory, and that's why we venerate it. So, we glory in the Cross. The devil has been defeated, and for this reason he is afraid of the Cross. It is the sign of his defeat.

Franciscus

Dear Pope Francis,

Good morning!
How can I find God in me and in my family? Bless me!

With Love,
Mansi

Age 9, India

Dear Pope Francis
Goodmorning!
How Can I find God in me and in my family? Bless me!

With Love
Mansi

Dear Mansi,

You can find God in your family by loving your mom, your dad, your brothers, your sisters, your grandpa, your grandma, and your aunts and uncles. If you love the people in your family, you will find God, and everything will be harmonious. And your drawing is like this—it's beautiful, serene, and harmonious. You are there, and I can tell that you are happy. You also have animals and plants. And there's your house. The doors are closed, but smoke is coming out of the chimney.

Love is not just the result of *your* actions. It is also a grace that you receive from God. And it is a grace that you have to help grow. You have to water it like you would water a plant. Every day learn to water the grace of love toward your family. Then you will find God in your home.

Franciscus

Dear Pope Francis,

I would like to find out why did God create us even though he knew that we would sin against him?

With love,
Maximus

Age 10, Singapore

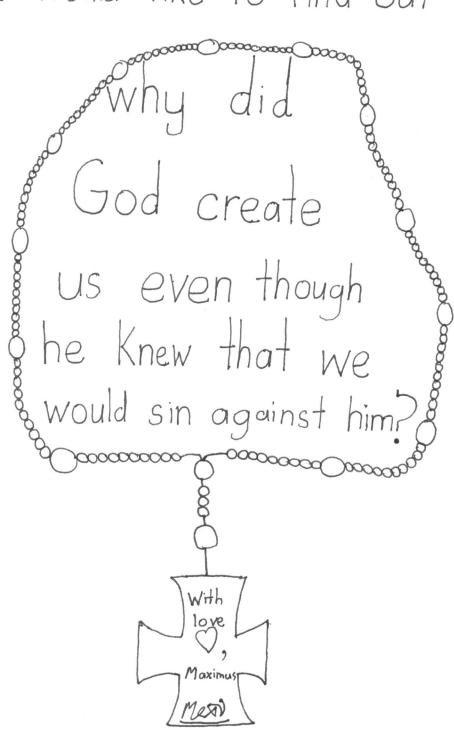

Dear Pope Francis,

I would like to find out why did God create us even though he knew that we would sin against him?

With love
♡,
Maximus

Maxi

Dear Maximus,

Because God has created us to be like himself. God created us to be free. Freedom is the greatest gift he has given us. Do you know that? And being free means we can choose to sin. But how many people are afraid of freedom! This is a serious problem today.

Many people are afraid of their own freedom and of other people's freedom. That's why some people prefer interacting with a pet that can give great affection, but it does not have the freedom another human being has. Freedom can scare people because it can't be programmed like a machine. And exactly for this reason, freedom is beautiful and God's greatest gift.

Franciscus

Dear Pope Francis,

I would like to ask you: is your profession hard, and were you liked, and who did you want to be at my age?

My name is Basia.
I am eight years old.
I like the color green.

Basia

Age 8, Poland

Drogi Papieżu Franciszku chciałabym zapytać Cię czy cięszki jest twój zawód i czy Byłeś lubiany i kim chciałeś zostać w moim wieku.

Nazywam się Basia mam 8 lat lubię kolor zielony.

Dear Basia,

I have to admit something. When I was your age,
I wanted to be a butcher. Now don't be astonished.
You know why? I used to go to the market with my
grandmother, and I'd see a butcher I liked. He was a
large fellow, and he had a long apron with a big pocket
in front. When my grandma would pay, he would put
his hands in the big pocket. It was full of money, and
he would give the change to my grandma. I thought he
was a very rich man. All this really affected me, and I
wanted to be like him. It's funny, but I have to confess
this to you.

Franciscus

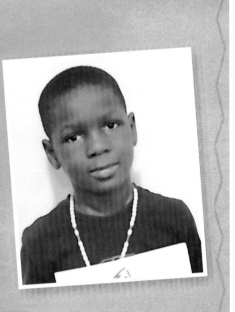

Dear Pope Francis,

How can you settle conflicts in the world?

Michael

Age 9, Nigeria

Dear Pope Francis, How can you settle conflicts in the world?

Michael

Dear Michael,

We have to help people of goodwill speak about war as something bad. The reason people wage war is to get more power and more money. The real cause of war is selfishness and greed. I can't resolve all the conflicts in the world, but you and I can try to make the earth a better place. People suffer, and even your drawing captures a sense of sadness. I can see that you know about conflict. But there is no magic wand. We have to convince everyone that the best way to win a war is not to wage one. I know that's not easy. But I'm going to try. And I ask you to try too.

Franciscus

Dear Pope Francis,

My name is Nastya. I live in Russia. This year I made my First Communion. I would like to ask you what I, as a child, can do to increase the number of Christians in my age group. Thank you. Goodbye.

Nastya

Age 10, Russia

Дорогой Папа римский - Франциск!
Меня зовут Настя. Я живу в России и в этом году я приняла первое причастие. Я хочу у вас спросить, что я как ребёнок могу сделать для того, чтобы возрастало количество христиан среди моих сверстников. Спасибо. До свидания.

Настя

Dear Nastya,

What a beautiful drawing! I can tell that you are used to seeing icons and praying with them! You really have a wonderful wish: to increase the number of those who love Jesus and who seek him. This is very beautiful. I support you. The best way to fulfill your wish is to pray to Jesus that the number of his followers will increase. And pray for pastors, for religious men and women, and for all those who proclaim the Gospel. But most of all, it's up to you! Give your witness as a Christian where you live, with your family, among your friends, and in your city. You have to be a witness of the faith that you hold in your heart. Pray and be a witness to the love of Jesus.

Franciscus

Dear Pope Francis,

1. Why do you need
   that tall hat?

2. Why do some saints
   have the wounds?

Faith
from Singapore

Age 8, Singapore

Dear Faith,

In your drawing, I have my tall hat, and your hair is blowing in the wind. We are hand in hand. Thank you for this wonderful picture! My tall hat is the symbol or sign that I am a bishop. I put it on for some special occasions and during Mass. Once in a while, I change it, but I like the one I had in Argentina, in Buenos Aires. When I would come to Rome before becoming pope, I would bring two hats: one all white for celebrations with the Pope and my other normal one for some celebrations I had here in Rome. And I still have that hat with me.

You also ask me about the wounds of the saints. Yes, some saints—like Saint Francis of Assisi—had the "stigmata," what we call the wounds of Jesus. These saints loved Jesus so much that they wanted to become like him. They wanted to imitate him. So Jesus gave them their gift: to have the same wounds as he had. In other words, they became like Jesus in their bodies. But be careful—not everyone who has wounds is a saint!

Franciscus

Dear Pope Francis,

Why are there not as many miracles anymore?

Joaquín

Age 9, Peru

Dear Joaquín,

Who told you this? It's not true! There are miracles even now. Every day there are miracles, and there are plenty of them. For example, there is the miracle of people who suffer and still do not lose their faith. So many people suffer and continue to remain faithful to Jesus. This is a miracle, a great miracle. I'm also thinking about our martyrs in the Middle East who are killed because they refuse to deny Jesus. This is another great miracle. And then, yes, there are healings.

But most of all there are everyday miracles—like the miracle of life and the miracle of good works that change people's hearts. You know that you can recognize them. I've experienced many miracles. No, they're not the spectacular kind. I have never seen the dead come back to life. But I have seen many daily miracles in my life. Many.

Franciscus

Dear Pope Francis,

If you could do one miracle what would it be?

Love,
William

Age 7,
United States of America

Dear Pope Francis,
If you could do 1 miracle what would it be?
Love,
William

Dear William,

I would heal children. I've never been able to understand why children suffer. It's a mystery to me. I don't have an explanation. I ask myself about this, and I pray about your question. Why do children suffer? My heart asks the question. Jesus wept, and by weeping, he understood our tragedies. I try to understand too. Yes, if I could perform a miracle, I would heal every child.

Your drawing makes me think: there is a big, dark cross, and a rainbow and the sunshine behind it. I like that. My answer to the pain of children is silence, or perhaps a word that rises from my tears. I'm not afraid to cry. You shouldn't be either.

Franciscus

Even small children have BIG questions

Delivering some very special letters to Pope Francis . . .

It's a hot August afternoon in Rome. I park my blue car in the shade of a building near Santa Marta. I enter the building and greet the Swiss Guard. I tell him that I have an appointment with the Holy Father. He says, "I know." With a wave of the hand, he invites me in. I enter and immediately am told that the Pope is waiting for me; I can go up. I regret having not come earlier. I take the elevator and press the button for the second floor. The doors open, and I seem to have made a mistake, so I press the button to the third floor. The doors open, and finally another Swiss Guard appears, smiling at me and not saying a thing.

"What do I do now?" I ask him. "Follow me," says the guard. And he invites me to knock on the door myself. There you go: what's more normal than knocking on a door, right? But it's Pope Francis's door. I see that the door is actually half open. I knock. I hear a voice from within but can't seem to hear what he's saying. I wait but peek through the crack. My curious eye meets the Pope's smiling face as he arrives and opens the door.

Faith
from: Singapore :))

I enter, we greet each other and talk. He remains standing and asks if I want something to drink, some water or some fruit juice. I tell him, "Water is fine." And he, smiling, asks, "Are you sure?" And I say, "No! Apricot juice, please." He had served me apricot juice two years before, after I had interviewed him for the magazine *La Civiltà Cattolica* and for other Jesuit magazines worldwide. "Great!" he says. "Gelato, yes or no?" "Gelato!" I say. The Pope opens a mini fridge and serves me. He has some water at room temperature for himself.

We sit down and begin to discuss many things. But I am here to speak on behalf of the children who, from various parts of the world, have posed questions and sent drawings to him. Yes, children from diverse Jesuit institutions in the world have written questions to Pope Francis, hoping to get an answer. They also sent him greetings and kisses. The Pope has agreed to answer thirty of the many questions that were sent. It would have been wonderful to answer them all; Pope Francis likes to answer children's questions.

I hand over the questions and drawings. The Pope is intrigued; he leafs through them, reads them, and then says, "But these are tough questions!"

"Indeed!" I had read them, and I also found them to be really difficult. The children's questions are unfiltered, no frills, with no way out. They are sharp, clear, even brusque. One can't escape into the shadow of highly abstract concepts or specious reasoning. These questions are also very practical.

> **"Our imaginations cannot help but travel to the places these children live."**

I switch on two recorders, and we begin. I know, I understand: the Pope would love to have these children in front of him. Pope Francis loves seeing the faces of the people who pose him questions. I have witnessed it many times. Now, however, he has only me in front of him, definitely not the face of a child. So I see that from time to time he looks off into space and answers a child whom he tries to imagine. He answers, not looking at me, but looking at the hypothetical image of Ryan, João, Nastya, Emil, Tom, Ivan . . . in his gaze I see care, fondness. I know that he is answering them in his heart. He tries to imagine them. He would love to have them here with him.

But I can't just sit still and *read* the questions. I identify with them. On this question or that one, I tell the Pope that I posed this very question to my mom. I am taken by his answers and at times ask a question again. At other times, I burst out laughing. Once I say, "How is that possible?" "You don't say!" In other words, I interact with the Pope, who interacts in his heart with the boy or girl who posed the question. A rather curious situation, but beautiful.

Pope Francis looks at the drawings. While answering, or after answering, he analyzes and interprets them; the drawing is part of the question. I note that, at times, the Pope captures, with his spiritual finesse, the meaning of a question more from the images than from the words that I read to him.

We spend an hour and a half like this without interruption. With him seated on the sofa and me in an armchair, our imaginations cannot help but travel to Canada, Brazil, Syria, China, Argentina, Albania . . . the places where these children live—beautiful gardens or refugee camps. We can grasp this from the drawings. At the end, I turn off my recorder. It's 5:30 p.m.

The Pope seems happy, but he clearly tells me what I had sensed: "It's beautiful to answer the questions of these children, but I should have them here with me, all of them!" I know that would be wonderful. But I also know that this book of responses will go into the hands of many children around the world who speak different languages. And for this I am happy.

I pick up the drawings, the recorder, my notes, and I finish my apricot juice. We chat for a little bit, and the Pope walks me to the elevator. I thank him for this time, and he looks at me, repeating what I already know: "Don't forget to pray for me." "I do this always," I say while the elevator doors close and I still bask for an instant in his smile.

Once home, transcribing the recording, it's as if I were doing a long meditation. I remember something that I heard the Pope say a while back in his speech to the general superiors of the religious orders: "It comes to mind when Paul VI received a letter from a little boy with many drawings. Paul VI said that, on the table where only letters with problems arrive, the arrival of this letter did him a lot of good. Tenderness does us good."

I realize that the language of Pope Francis is simple and that he lives in simple words. Because God is simple. The tenderness of God is revealed in his simplicity. One must not complicate God, especially if this complication distances God from the people. God is with us, and to be really with us, he has to be simple. The presence of a person is simple. Even the physical presence of Pope Francis has the flavor of simplicity. And this flavor is also in the most profound things he says, as in these responses to the children. I am sure of this: Pope Francis's responses to these questions will do good for all, and especially for those who refuse to become simple like children.

Antonio Spadaro, S.J.
Director of La Civiltà Cattolica

Pope Francis with Fr. Spadaro

Papal Pen Pal Facts

Children took no time at all coming up with their questions for Pope Francis. They swiftly responded with letters and drawings that ranged from the fun to the serious, the curious to the profound. When holding the letters in his hands for the first time, Pope Francis smiled and said, "These questions are tough!"

By the numbers:

- **259 letters received**

- **From 26 countries**

- **From 6 continents**

- **Written in 14 languages**

- **Gathered with the help of dozens of willing volunteers**

One lesson learned: Children are trying to make sense of the world, and they look to us adults to help them. Pope Francis showed his profound love and respect for the children by making time to listen, to see, and to respond from his heart. He has the heart of a shepherd who cares deeply for his tender flock.

Letters from Chil

dren around the World

Love and Gratitude

This book was a project of love for all who participated, including His Holiness, Pope Francis, who eagerly awaited the children's letters and responded to them from his heart, and also Antonio Spadaro, S.J., a very busy man who nonetheless arranged for the meeting with Pope Francis and who transcribed Pope Francis's responses. The Loyola Press team, too many people to list, also embraced this project with joy and gladness.

Love and gratitude go to:

- Each of the children who shared his or her question and drawing. Every one of the letters submitted was bundled into one volume and presented to Pope Francis.

- Every child who reads this book on his or her own or with a parent, grandparent, older sibling, teacher, or other caring person. Know that your questions are good and can lead you to God. You should trust those questions to people who love you and want the very best for you.

Here is a list of the Jesuit priests and their lay colleagues who gathered letters from more than 250 children from every region of the world.

Albania: Zef Bisha, S.J.; **Argentina:** Elisabetta Piqué; **Australia:** Elizabeth Kaye, Richard Leonard, S.J.; **Belgium:** John Dardis, S.J., Philip Debruyne, S.J.; **Brazil:** Eduardo Henriques, S.J., Antonio Tabosa, S.J.; **Canada:** Frank Obrigewitsch, S.J., Jeannine Pistawka; **China:** Irene Cheung, Stephen Chow, S.J., Louis Gendron, S.J., Emmanuel Lim, S.J., Rachel Xiaohong Zhu; **Dominican Republic:** Jose Victoriano, S.J.; **India:** Sunny Jacobs, S.J., George Pattery, S.J., Robert Slattery, S.J.; **Ireland:** Laoise Breathnach, Pat Coyle; **Italy:** Patrick Mulemi, S.J., Giovanni Notari, S.J.; **Kenya:** Sr. Victorine Nyang'or, IBVM; **Netherlands:** Nikolaas Sintobin, S.J.; **Nicaragua:** Ruth Albuquerque, Julie Falbo, Kathleen McBride; **Nigeria:** Very Reverend Father Hyacinth Ogbodo, CSSp, Deacon Lawrence R. Sutton, PhD; **Peru:** Oscar Morelli, S.J.; **Philippines:** Karen Goh, Mari Bianca Orenciana; **Poland:** Przemek Mąka, S.J.; **Portugal:** Ana Guimaraes; **Russia:** Stefan Lipke, S.J.; **Singapore:** Mark Aloysius, S.J., Julie Phua; **Spain:** Juan Carlos Manso Pérez; **Syria:** Tony Homsy, S.J.; **United Kingdom:** Ruth Morris, Cathy Poloczek; **United States of America:** Fr. Louis J. Cameli, Beth Carroll, Pat Casey, S.J., Elisa Ciaglia, Beatrice Ghislandi, Gary Jay, Mary Larkin, Chris Lowney, Yvonne Micheletti, Gary Smith, S.J., George Witt, S.J.; **Zimbabwe:** Joseph Arimoso, S.J.

Tom McGrath

Tom McGrath
Director, Trade Books, Loyola Press